SAFE HOUSE

Iggy McGovern

DEDALUS PRESS
DUBLIN, IRELAND

ACKNOWLEDGEMENTS

Acknowledgements are due to the editors of the following in which a number of these poems, or versions of them, originally appeared: *A Treasury of Sunday Miscellany, An Sionach (USA), College Green, Magdalen Record (UK), Poetry Ireland Review, Southword* and *Turbine (NZ)*.

The author wishes to thank the Ireland Chair of Poetry Trust for a residency at the Tyrone Guthrie Centre in Annaghmakerrig and La Trobe University for a fellowship at the Institute for Advanced Study.

First published in 2010 by
The Dedalus Press
13 Moyclare Road
Baldoyle
Dublin 13
Ireland

www.dedaluspress.com

ISBN 978 1 906614 34 8

Dedalus Press titles are represented in North America by
Syracuse University Press, Inc., 621 Skytop Road,
Suite 110, Syracuse, New York 13244,
and in the UK by
Central Books, 99 Wallis Road, London E9 5LN

Cover image by Pat and Lee Boran

The Dedalus Press receives financial assistance from
The Arts Council / An Chomhairle Ealaíon

BB

SAFE HOUSE

for Una and Martin

Contents

I

II. Letters from The Captain

III

I

Utterance

It wasn't the Salmon of Knowledge,
though all the neighbours knew its source
in that chauffeur-driven Daimler.

The spoil of the Colonel's river sport
lay on our stoop, one glass eye glaring
from yesterday's *Telegraph*.

Somewhere between the generous
and the feudal lies a mother's lack
of a big enough cooking pot.

And somewhere there is a growing boy
telling the whole world he prefers
his salmon from the tin.

The Cartographers

We are making a giant map of our town
in Primary School in 'fifty-seven,
dividing the task into sixteen squares
of white cardboard, two pupils per card.
When all the cards have been collected
and pinned together on the blackboard
we suddenly see that Railway Road
has been detached from Kingsgate Street;
there's no way through to the Town Hall
from Stone Row, a complete dead end.
And someone, possibly the boy
who will do time for Ireland, says:
*Please Sir, it looks as if a bomb
has gone off in our town.*

Climbing Croagh Patrick

We have things to talk about
man to man, that's why
I'm scrabbling up this stony slope
under a doubtful sky.

> Weaned within sound of the bell
> of the Anglican church—St. Patrick's!—
> I grew up believing you were
> Protestant as well:
> I had you banishing the snakes
> with the same bleak certainty
> that pitched the monks in the river
> and planted the best of the County.

A rest at the First Station.
For seven-fold penance I recall
my seven years' re-education:
you were Catholic, after all.

> We'd a great day out on Slemish
> for our Patrician Ceremonies,
> fifteen hapless centuries
> of your Mission to the Irish.
> Of which I remember only
> the Union Jacks all along the route
> (reminders that they held you yet)
> and sweet, scalding tea.

On top I join the tourists
hugging the chapel gable
enveloped in sacred mists,
a rain-swept tower of Babel.

I strike my bell to summon
from the vaults of the Old School,
swaddled in cotton-wool,
your One, True Jawbone
that once in a one-bulb room
I questioned closely, slapping
its toothless, brown half-grin:
Whose side are you on?

It was all a waste of time.
We saints are trained to say
nothing. Except that in a better clime
you must have a great view of Clew Bay.

The Child of Prague

Lookout on the windowsill,
hard man with the babyface,
the runaway whose only speech
was "pray-ig"… Over there they still
exchange your smocks of rich brocade,
the way a mother might do up
the buttons on a Burberry, lace
small shoes, before the agitprop's
child-soldiery for the one true cause.
Patron saint of the safe house,
you turned a deaf ear to the screech
of tyres late into the night,
vestments cloaking armalite,
orb, a hand-grenade.

The Religious Question

for Martin

They seemed uneasy neighbours then,
Public House and Protestant Church
facing across the broad main street.
A child of eight,
clearing glasses from the snug
I'd catch a slow wet funeral
or sun-bright wedding party
funneling through the gates.

Almost forty years before
I step inside, surprised how small
it is. The leaflet says: Welcome!
The Volunteers'
drum beats no alarum,
no flutter of interest from
the war-torn Union flags,
the eagle's unblinking eye.

The leaflet bids me pray for …
who else but 'The Soldier',
marching ramrod past our house
each Sunday morning
noosed in his regimental tie,
'King James' under his arm,
blood-shot eyes front
for The Second Coming.

And pray for his alter ego,
the Saturday night commando
dropped behind the enemy lines
of small-town temperance.
His tour of duty over,
curfewed by closing time,
he rambles home but, first,
his *nunc dimittis:*

propped against our garden gate
he chants plainsong my father's name
over and over, as if it were
some holy mantra,
calming him, meditative,
a gathering of his strength
to ask the street, the town, the world:
"What do they want?"

Incident

for Noel

'Liquorice-legs' was what we called
each well-heeled daughter of The Union
in belted Burberry of emerald green
"the highest colour in the Orange Lodge!"
Venus on stilts of black.

Our daily homeward march went past
their High School, with its netball courts,
the jolly smack of hockey sticks,
our only game the leap to snatch
the trophy-scalp beret.

"What the hell were you thinking of?"
(sex, of course, though not by name).
It could have been a tipping point:
curfew, reprisal, pogrom … instead
we were forcibly re-routed.

Anthem

for Peter

Matinée at The Palace,
the hero rides into the sunset;
unwilling to run the gauntlet
of Protestant elbow and knee,
we stay for the red line of soldiers,
the lipstick of royal grimace.
Back home in Princess Gardens
my father turns off the television
at the first roll of the drums
and launches into The Rosary.
We kneel at kitchen chairs,
hearing the faint refrain,
da-da-da-da "send her victorious",
seeping into the house.

Good neighbours, till July
brings out the Twelfth marchers,
to The Field and back, the worse
for speeches, Brother Alcohol
and paper pokes of chips,
straightening up for a final
"happy and glorious".
We said they were only loyal
to the half-crown, just like us,
taking grants and scholarships.
But once in the Old Town Hall
when the tune was part of the play,
the audience didn't hesitate
and leapt to their feet.

Weekend-working in bars,
home from college, the trick
at closing time was how much
we could drink out of sight before
the resident band would reach
"Long to reign over us".
Then chasing after romance
in halls where we didn't belong,
juking in for the last dance
of a Ceili and then the craic—
up twice within the hour,
this time for 'The Soldier's Song',
heads flung back, voices slurred,
pretending to know the words.

It was all the one to us
and whichever one holds sway
we stand, and maybe recall
that every Christmas Day
there was a kind of truce.
After the Pope's Blessing
we re-tuned for Her Message,
saying "she has her troubles"
and "isn't she nicely dressed?"
while shifting our unease
with some crack about her dogs—
"Is it time for Urbi et Corgis?"—
and whispering back to the screen
"God Save The Queen".

The Women in the Moon

The first has no time, so it seems,
for silver apples: she must put
the food on plates, the clothes on backs.
Her apples are the giant cookers
boiled in sugar, oozing through
the fork-indented crusts of tarts
where you might find a ring, a sixpence
tissue-wrapped in mother's love,
and, when it waxes sickle-bright,
your wish comes true.

The second is ahead of you
in everything: you tag along
unwanted on the expeditions
to pick bluebells for her May altar.
But she minds you in the backlane,
brave big sister pulling hair
so hard their eyes blink back the tears,
and teaches you the nursery rhymes:
'The Cow Jumped Over...', 'Mother Goose',
'Old Aiken Drum'.

The third redeems you from the thrum
of city-bars and one-night stands:
man and wife, sweet joy in tide,
but soon you're scratching at the window,
baying at the crazed eclipse,
this "monster swallowing the source".
She knows, of course, what must be done
to save the day: bang on the drum,
on pots and pans and softly cry
"Hullaballoo".

The fourth is merely waiting to
complete the quartet that the heavens
fling into your orbit: she
will always be your little girl,
red apple cheeks and bluebell eyes,
and when she grows you'll be the one
to sit up till the cows come home,
complaining, watching for the goose-
drawn chariots that ferry her
hither, thither.

Return to the Rose Garden

for my mother

Slip the straps of the satchel
to join in the game,
circling the slow sundial,
chanting each rose's name.

The Festival of Britain.
Peacetime. Soon the town
will toast the new Queen:
Piccadilly, Gold Crown...

You have come to live
at ease among the Saxon
gone (almost) native:
Wheatcroft, Granpa Dixon...

The Graingers, Gaults and Goughs,
Jazz on their radios;
miracle of sliced loaf;
Sunblest, Satchmo...

Chill in the evening air;
the parkman's jangling keys
invite a grateful prayer:
Coleraine, Peace...

The Eleven-Plus

The night before the examination
my mother sewed the Miraculous Medal
into my trouser pocket.
I entered the foreign state
of the County Intermediate School
armed with a new fountain-pen.
It was Friday—was it a trap
to serve up fish for lunch?
Carefully washing my hands
I wrote in my very best alias
about my pals in the Library
(Julian, Dick, Anne and George)
while my address slowly faded
in lemon juice.

The Dress Rehearsal

The wicker hamper yields real swords,
an instant knuckle-skinning chase,
then doublet, hose, a martial cloak,
King Henry's crown and half-league boots
for young Prince Ger and Falstaff Jim
and our best hurler Hotspur Pat.
But, soft, the Ladies Mortimer
and Percy enter—a giggling brace
of Junior boys in rustling skirts
with frilly lace about the bosom.
All night they tripped the corridors,
dropped scented kerchiefs in their wake,
peeped round my dormitory partitions,
crooking finger invitations.

Belfast Inequalities

for Master Devlin

Who put the pie in Pythagoras,
who put the bra in algebra,
and who was the first to say: Let x
be that unknown quantity in sex?
The answer's in some chromosome
and not the sums you do at home
to win at Spot-The-Ball, for by
the time you get to take away
the number you first started with
the best lookin' girls in Lower Fifth
are gone. And when will you understand
that half a loaf is better than
no bread? But round here everyone says:
No Bread Is Better Than Kennedy's!

Suburban Grimm

for Mererid

It wasn't our resident fairy godmother
stretched out on the lounger, complaining the garden
had magicked itself into such a deep forest
that Hansel & Gretel were yesterday's stew;
and it wasn't Rapunzel above in the bathroom—
the mirror wisely still taking The Fifth—
while her sister Snow White talks for hours on the phone
to a pimple-pocked prince with the lips of a frog;
and it wasn't the flies, which I killed by the sevens,
that occasioned my Rumpelstiltskinny war-dance:
it was merely the door bell kept ringing and ringing
and no one would answer. And what do I see
but a crew cut, tooth-perfect young stranger from Utah
who's asking me three simple questions, just three!

Suburban Commute

Christus in der Schlagwitze Kirche

Here is the Christ I ought to love,
not the child in mother's arms
or the local hero out to prove
himself, whatever the harm.
He could sit on a railway bench,
the left arm lost like one bad thief,
the right by force of habit glued
from knee to hand-cupped chin.
Search those eyes for any belief
other than that the eight-ten will
shortly arrive at Platform Two,
the signal that he should begin
to lift his paper and packed lunch
and climb that hill.

Suburban Sanbenito*

Mostly I'm content with yellow,
signed and sealed, a pot scraped clean,
easily yoked to the shopping trolley,
arms outstretched for the winding wool,
all squeezy-bottled up in the kitchen.
Excitement? Whipping the powercord
out of the lawnmower's path.

But sometimes on warm summer evenings
when the carnival comes to town
and the music drifts from over the river,
I get the urge for black,
the embrace of painted devils
to end it all, screaming profanities
into the bonfired air.

* Corruption of 'Saint Benedict';
  a penitential garment of the Inquisition

The Mower

i.m. John McKernan

Bamfords (Uttoxeter),
when we last met
(that glorious summer
in well-named Rushhill)
I wasn't the height
of your chariot wheels,

all clatter and hum
in a gun-metal grey,
revealing by turns
the shuttling blade:
"Thon laddie's tongue
would soon pare your corns".

My good uncle's caustic
countryman's wit,
a poet-mechanic
bent over the task
of replacing a bolt
newly fashioned in brass.

Rushlight among rust,
a faith-keeping beacon
resurrecting The Just.
Look, he's back in the seat,
trailing clouds of Sweet Afton;
for the second, sweet cut.

Last Rites

Bringing my father to the barber's,
an old-style place with blood-let pole,
the terrace marked for development,
I'm thinking how slow he has become
when he tells a joke: "D'you know what were
the two flies at on a bald man's pate?
They were playing," he pauses to inhale,
"playing at hide-and-seek!"
Inside, they make a fuss of him;
he jumps the queue, his case is urgent.
Released at last with knowing looks,
I link him along the wasted street:
just one hesitant step ahead
of the bulldozer's tread.

Imagine, give or take a day,
four weeks after the funeral
the local Board chiropodist
turns up to treat my father's feet
(he'd been waiting for a year).
My mother greets him with her fist
and hunts him from the door.
Her anger giving way to humour
is preferable to my irony's
dull ache, like an ingrown nail,
which has me staring up the street
and wondering who might next appear:
the butcher, the baker,
the candlestick-maker?

When the cards came from the printers
I snipped the string, and caught my breath
as they fanned across the tablecloth,
face down like a brand new deck.
Gathering a handful close to my chest,
I cut and dealt unending pairs.
For he was a legend in church halls,
The Pigeon Club, The British Legion,
Top Score Gent in any school.
Once he tried to teach me whist
but all I did was 'box the pack';
and now I sit like some magician
sealing a card that speaks of Hope
into a black-edged envelope.

The Naming of Swanlinbar

The single swan in Swanlinbar's
no more a clue than the first curacy
of my father in one of its bars;

likewise the Irish (though not entirely)
An Muileann Iarainn for Swanlinbar,
meaning The Iron Factory ...

Picture instead four entrepreneurs
from the early part of the 18th century
setting up a riverside foundry: Messrs

Swift, Sanders, Darling and Barry,
concocting the name of Swandlingbar
in furnace-melded formulary.

Sacraments

1. SELKIE

for Slim Jim

Relict of a naughty postcard,
deckchair sprawler on a rock,
you're *The Fat Boy, Bunter, Lard,*
last man round the old school track.
Until we're taken out to learn
to swim: our jumping off the side
sets up a maelstrom. Spray 'n' churn
have barely settled when you dive.
Instead of belly-flopping foam,
we witness mirror-finish calm,
as if the water were your home
and on this silent entering
becomes the pool at Siloam,
brushed by an angel's wing

2. THE JOEY TRINITY

for Una

There were three budgies in one Joey
co-equal but not co-existing:
the first taught wisdom through experience,
seizing the chance of an open door
to ascend into heaven;
the second took after Father Peyton,
setting up a crusading racket,
joyful, sorrowful, glorious by turns
during the family rosary;
the third *mirabile dictu* learned
to say his name, the word made flesh,
and had the courage to crash-land
on Dad's bald head, occasioning
some tongues of fire.

3. THE CURATE'S EGG

When Sunday morning Mass is done
the Curate ambles to the door
of Aunt Kay's house: breakfast for one.

The Good Room, folding table spread
with linen, china, Apostle spoon,
tea cosy and two kinds of bread.

The kitchen is a powder keg
where Aunt Kay labours to create
the ideal, the perfect fried egg.

Sausage and bacon mouth dismay
as each flawed sunnyside is chucked
(the village dogs will have their day).

The Father's Love is just and meet.
Aunt Kay breaks fast in His Good Room.
The Curate labours in the heat.

4. NOT ROWING BUT

Forgive me, we had barely met
(blame the wine, the midday heat);
you were rowing, I was steering
but really I was rudely staring,
gawking like some adolescent
down your cleavage, oscitant
in the oars' sweep to and fro,
my River Belle peep-show.

If only I had kept them there,
not raised my eyes to higher up:
your face has that I'm-gone-elsewhere
look, tell-tale, half-bitten lip,
the O-don't-quit-on-me-now frown
and I almost drown.

5. THE WEAPON-SALVE

'...that like the weapon-salve, heals at a distance'
— *The Young King* (1690) by Aphra Behn

Like the ancients I confess
that I can never quite dismiss
the weapon-salve, the balm applied
to that which caused the cut.
Tonight I'll crawl back to anoint
the eyes that failed to see the point,
the ears that could not be believed,
the nostrils that had smelt a rat,
the mouth that queried *who* and *what,*
the hands that would be washed of it,
the feet that took their leave
and further dare the fructified
wound-weapon of our battlefield
and hope to wake up, healed.

6. MELCHIZEDEK

I liked him, he had the family look,
Adam's apple prominent
above the Roman collar,
and his eyes didn't follow you
around the room.
He disappeared sometime in the spring:
they all pretended not to hear
when I asked where he'd gone.
I found him, quite by accident,
face down in a drawer upstairs.
He came to visit, brought photographs:
a wife and family, somewhere foreign.
Marking orders old and new,
we name him Father Pat-That-Was.

7. Ode to a Green Shopping Bag

for Eileen

A fashion statement of the modern man
where green is the new black, its warp and weft
of see-u-out extended lifetime span
soft-handled but still equal to the heft.
Each Saturday it nestles in the boot
beside the golf clubs, eager to be filled
with caviar, blue cheese and passion fruit,
a long-lived Sauterne ready to be chilled.

Yet I recall another time afresh
when plastic bags were strewn like autumn leaves
before their banishment by dour experts:
the handles almost cutting through my flesh,
three flights of stairs, your flat beneath the eaves,
the gas fire, narrow bed, our just desserts.

The Five-Day Break

1. ARRIVAL

O happy accident to have discovered
The Grand Hotel, the kind of place where gents
will don a jacket and tie for Dinner,
and waiters dance around on tippy-toes
with trays of hall-marked silver and good delft.
Authentic re-creation of 'The Big House'
where your grandfather was head gardener,
his child—your mother—buffing each stair-rod
till she could see in it the very face
you meet these days at every turn-about:
here, playing Patience on the sunny terrace;
there, linked as far as this low seaside-fence,
now threatening a round of Crazy Golf
if it keeps good, before the week is out.

2. MARINER

Alas, there's not an even chance that he
will this time only stoppeth one of three:
the beach is empty, it's too late for joggers
and much too early for the odd day-tripper.
He cuts across your path with measured tread,
his eye fixed on your tell-tale writing pad.
You're trapped between the 18-hole golf course
and the deep blue. Yes, he composes verse:
"O limericks and the like", reciting one
and then another, and, yes, he's been on
the radio. You tell him you have miles
to go. He shrugs. He knows only too well
you will avoid him, take the long road back,
his burning thirst for fame hung round your neck.

3. Sunburn

Just like the morning after drunken sex,
you tell yourself you should have known better.
Fitting punishment for yesterday's
ungracious treatment of a fellow writer:
"Yo, lobsterman, all hail tomato-rex".
Your skin as tight as a tourniquet
you limp into the nearby pharmacy,
familiar scene of old embarrassments,
remembering the first time that you bought
a packet of, er, you know what? "What? WHAT!"
And now you lie embalmed in zinc-based cream
like scorched Massala in his loser's tent
and summon up a rasping silent scream:
O don't you, don't you even dare touch me!

4. SAND

Out on the beach before the local heroes
to gently break-in yesterday's sunburn,
you leap with ease across a castle ruin—
a Gulliver trapped in egg-timer land—
that, ere the sun hath set, an outsize hand
will fee-fie-fo-fum rudely overturn
and set you to the Sisyphean job
of registering each and every grain
upon an abacus of tiny shells.
Such number-crunching forces you to pose
the ancient riddle that might break the spell:
"Whatever shall we do for micro-chips
when all the silicon has been used up?"
The answer right there, at your toe-tips?

5. DEPARTURE

And suddenly, too soon, it is all over;
assorted luggage piled up in the hall
reminding you, unseasonably, of Christmas,
the breaking up for hols from boarding school
or that bleak ritual at Midnight Mass:
"And who can know for sure which of us won't
be sitting in these seats this time next year?"
It's time instead for you to pay your dues,
to mail the postcards to your maiden aunts
and slip a sideways tenner to your waiter,
load up the car and make some weak excuse
to take one last look back along the strand
and trace with dragging feet in giant letters:
IT WAS GRAND.

II

Letters from The Captain

for Zenia

My maternal grandfather, Andrew (Andy) McHugh, was head gardener to Seskinore House in County Tyrone. In late 1938 his employer, a Captain Joynson-Wreford, was airlifted to a TB clinic in Davos, where he would die shortly after the outbreak of war. Over the intervening months he wrote weekly to my grandfather, ordering the affairs of the estate, requesting personal items to be forwarded, and providing a moving remembrance of his abandoned home; his beloved wife ,'The Mistress', had pre-deceased him and was buried in the grounds of the house. My grandfather and his family lived in the house for a short time. When The Captain died, his daughter, 'Miss Xenia', was fostered, spending much of her adult life in Australia; she did not return to her home place until some 60 years later. Seskinore House was billeted with American soldiers during the war, and was demolished shortly afterwards.

1. Flight

'PLANE AS AMBULANCE' the caption read
above the group around the striped tailfin.
The Captain sitting on his stretcher-bed
smiles bravely for the newsman's Rollei-twin.

The early morning sun is Easter bright
as Army colleagues wish him all the best.
Miss Xenia is somewhere out of sight;
the nurse is young and fashionably dressed.

The pilot tells her not to be afraid.
From Barnstaple to Zurich? Half a day!
The groundsman hauls on the propeller blade,
retiring with the shouted "chocks away!"

And as the fragile aircraft gathers height,
who feels the 'lonely impulse of delight'?

2. HOUSE SITTING

(Grandfather)

And who'd have thought that this would come to pass:
the gardener standing in the master's stead,
the bathroom with a wall-length looking-glass,
the curtains on the great four-poster bed.

The Missus claims their ghosts are everywhere.
She swears we won't get out of here alive:
the weeping child ascending the half-stair,
the midnight coach-and-four raked down the drive.

We shun the good rooms, keep our proper place
before the range in borrowed easy chairs.
What would I give to see the Colonel's face
if he were witness to our 'Roman' prayers?

As in 'the trimmins'*, ghost and man are blessed.
God grant us, high and low, a good night's rest.

* *Special intentions for family and friends added to the family rosary*

3. THE MISTRESS' GARDEN

A shady spot beneath the laurel tree,
her birthday falling just in Whitsuntide;
Grandfather hard at work down on one knee,
a daughter, Cis or Kitty, by his side.

Go back two years, and, when it's time to quit,
hide in the bushes, then you're bound to catch
The Captain and a dog, her favourite,
as they begin their solitary watch.

Six decades on, Grandfather long deceased,
The Captain by The Mistress' side at last,
marked by these matching stones, and from the East
Miss Xenia journeys back to claim her past.

A simple latch, no barring chain or lock,
a rueful invitation to 'please knock'.

4. TULIPS

(The Captain)

They say the Dutchman once prepared for war
to keep his national interest in this flower.
The whole of Europe now in thrall to Thor
could fall upon itself within the hour.

The nurses opened Andy's box with care.
The pretty German-speaking one exclaimed:
"Die Blumen, Sie sind schon, nicht wahr, Mein Herr?"
I noted how the frost had left them maimed.

For what was she to know of Seskinore,
the tulips massing on the lower lane:
the very sight of them left me heartsore
and longing to be back at home again.

Soon GI's will arrive in serried ranks
and crush the roadside tulips with their tanks.

5. THE UMBRELLA

(The Captain)

Arrived today, first post, without a scratch
(well packed by Andy, just as he'd been told);
at once unfurled, it seemed that I might catch
the New Year bidding farewell to the Old.

Duck-handled, royal colours, wooden tines,
my loyal friend—perhaps my *fascio*
as when, flushed from The Major's vintage wines
I judged the floral wreaths at Omagh Show—

and with me at a time that will not fade,
the darkest hour of that unhappy day;
my best supporter when we gently laid
The Mistress in the undeserving clay.

Be with me now, in all that lies ahead—
my boon companion, when all hope is fled.

6. The Outing

(Grandfather)

The Captain was, of course, good as his word:
two tickets, post haste, for the Omagh Show,
the Grand Enclosure, decent seats assured.
Too grand, perhaps—the Missus wouldn't go!

So Bob and I set off to catch the train
from Fintona, all in our Sunday best.
I checked I had the tickets time and again,
a "Captain Joynson-Wreford and his guest".

And Bob would have us drink a glass of stout.
I'd just the one, it gives me stomach pains.
We landed home before the day was out,
my pockets full of sweeties for the weans,

a silk scarf for the Missus; in my head
thoughts of The Captain in his hospice bed.

7. WAR

(The Captain)

I heard the grim news on the radio,
the last lot was enough for any man.
What mindless blood-lust drives this stupid show?
The Swiss, at least, will stay out if they can.

I can't stay here, will have to face the flak
and go to London, get Miss Xenia out
to safety. It's clear we should come back,
for even now I seriously doubt

if Mister Hitler has a mind to send
his troops to Fivemiletown or Sixmilecross.
The poet caught it nicely when he penned
the line: 'No likely end could bring them loss.'

But even there, some things will not remain:
small courtesies of life, my lost demesne.

8. Two Cars

The first, the touring vehicle consummate,
the "S.S." with its lamps and cooling grids.
They wave The Captain off in thirty-eight
en route to Cairo's Hotel Pyramids.

When, barely two years on, the car is sold,
the Customs men come looking for their booty,
Le Carnet de Passage, M'sieur is told.
There may be war but they will have their duty!

The second is Miss Xenia's pedal-car,
with proper steering-wheel that worked a charm.
Tan-coloured with red trim and toy tow-bar,
it came down to the cousins on the farm.

I found it in the turf shed. For a treat
they waved me off as I roared down the street.

9. THE PHEASANTS

They perch upon a papier-mâché rock,
eternal calm before the beater's cry,
retrievers, plus-fours, cartridge-belt and stock,
both barrels peppering the autumn sky.

The taxidermist, Williams of Dame Street,
recalls to still life feather, beak and claw
(rare bird himself where Art and Science meet,
also a celebrated concert draw.)

Observers of the Big House rise and fall,
bought for ten shillings at the closing sale,
willed on to us, as if in answered call,
and once again they take the southern trail.

The well-worn ties of time and place are loosed
as more than these two birds come home to roost.

III

The Irish Poem Is

a Táin Bó, a Spring Show, a video
a trodden dream, a parish team, a tax-break scheme
a prison cell, an Angelus bell, a clientele
a brinded cow, a marriage vow, a domestic row
a tattered coat, a puck goat, a telly remote
a game of tig, a slip jig, a U2 gig
a restored tower, a Holy Hour, a pressure shower
a ticking clock, a summer frock, a shock-jock
a hazel wand, a dipping pond, a page 3 blonde
a canal bank, a returned Yank, a septic tank
a green flag, a Child of Prague, a Prada bag
a whispering sea, a Rose of Tralee, a transfer fee
a disused shed, a settle bed, a Club Med
a long strand, a ceili band, a one night stand
a 'barbaric yawp', a sweet shop, an alcopop
a flax dam, a high pram, an email spam
a new estate, a blind date, a security gate
a pint of plain, a lover's lane, a place in Spain
a cold eye, a bittern cry, a heroin high
a Raglan Road, a tractor load, a Da Vinci code
a lake isle, a wooden stile, a paedophile
a night feed, a Rosary bead, a corporate greed
a lonely impulse, a bag of dulse, a fading pulse
a herring shoal, a fox stole, a death toll
a Pangur Bán, a paraffin can, a fake tan
a fire-king, a fairy ring, a bling-bling
a tickled trout, a boy scout, a ticket tout
a wild swan, a frogspawn, a roll-out lawn
a lost tribe, a Tara Street scribe, a planning bribe
a huge rose, a garden of repose, a wine nose
a hedgehog, a peat bog, a weblog

a whirlpool, a milking stool, a drug mule
a stony grey soil, a three-in-one oil, a Mrs. Doyle
a planter's daughter, a school jotter, a mineral water
a potato pit, a banana-split, a gangland hit
a deep heart's core, a Georgian door, a quick score
a newborn lamb, a radiogram, an internet scam
a village master, a sticking plaster, a ghetto blaster
a third light, a second sight, a bungalow blight
a solitary enzyme, a closing time, an end rhyme.

Annaghmakerrig Haiku

i.m. Eithne McGuinness

Annaghmakerrig:
The house is known by the trees.
Fortnight of Sundays.

Shooting rights preserved
pour encourager les autres:
two holes in the sign.

The kitchen's back door
one-gun salute announcing
comings and goings.

Loch Eanach Mhic Dheirg:
smoothing the ruffled feathers
a fly-past of swans.

Guthrie's picnic place,
creak of the wicker basket,
no shred of litter.

Doohat Post Office:
is it my accent or these
large brown envelopes?

The dining table:
passing plates and fresh remarks—
'the garlic-eaters'.

Guitar recital.
Marco's dress shirt bleeds red wine.
Eithne rubs in salt.

The drawing room fire,
lashings of un-ginger beer,
the Shecret Sheven.

The bus timetable,
a new face at the window,
the lift into town.

The Anglers of Annaghmakerrig

after 'Fishing Around' by Robert Mezey

So many poems have tackled this before:
the poet fishing for *bon mot*, the small
fry-phrase thrown back with curses from the shore ...
But from their ranks it's easy to recall
the sonnet where close listening is repaid
in one line. Was it even planned?
'To please you, *lovely reader, meter made*'
(O yeah, somebody's lonely hearts club band).

The anglers muse in silence, bar a nod
of greeting to the poets, tend their patch
of lake, its surface speckled with small birds.
Beyond the reach of fountain pen or rod
both sides agree that catching beats the catch,
but only one will have to eat their words.

Peregrine

for Jonathan

Your silly public schoolboy name
belies your nature, hired gun.
When we surprised you at your lunch
you rose so fast that only a *whoosh*
betrayed you, that and these remains
of a homing pigeon—its good race run,
the owner's contact number grained
on one wing-feather. "When the call came…"

All this within view of the Rathlin East Light
and the concrete stumps that mark Marconi's
hi-tech reply to your dawn raid:
Lloyds' carrier pigeons, easy meat.
You eye from afar the mobile phone,
wait for the signal to fade.

Epigone

for Gerald Dawe

O Ulster, University, The New…
(the brutal seventies had just begun),
small world, indeed, and yet we barely knew
each other, on our separate fox's runs,
yours Protestant and Internationalist,
mine Catholic and small 'u' Unionist!

On top of which another border lay,
a different kind of 'two cultures' divide:
Arts versus Science, with no middle way,
begun in school, A-Level certified.
I cleaved to Newton and *The Time Machine*
while you chose Shakespeare and *The Faerie Queene!*

Perhaps we mingled in The Anchor Bar's
high temple, priested by the Currid Boys.
While lower orders seek their avatars
amid The Sea Splash Disco's rutting noise,
we settle for experience that endures:
a good book, and a takeout from McClure's!

But, not content with mastering the canon,
you have to write your own poems, hang around
with those real Honest Ulstermen, The London-
Derry and Alpha now your stomping ground.
Imaginary circles woven thrice,
opaque to my mere optical device!

Well, here we are now thirty-two or -three
years after … marriage, children, and alive …
The Holy 'n' Undivided Trinity
anoints us fellow Fellows as we strive
to teach the under-whelmed and oversexed,
displaying their deft thumbnail grasp of 'text'!

And here at last we ponder the revealed
significance of Brooke's old comfiture
that there's some corner of a foreign field
that is forever English Literature:
your Centre stands in Snovian defiance
amid the test-tubes and lab-coats of Science!

We'd say 'unstable equilibrium'
or even joke about the catalyst
among the pigeons. Ante prandium
some hybrid breed of Poet-Scientist
might crawl out of this cauldron of pitch-blende:
your epigone and—steady on!—your friend.

Louis MacNeice at *The Original Print Gallery*

for Crona

He takes the train to Dublin—Enterprise
is evident, The Spire, smart new trams.
Relieved to find 'much history never dies',
he mourns the old street traders with the prams.

Boston? Berlin? New Irish everywhere,
'toy Liffey' sports a chic boardwalk café.
He lingers to breathe in this foreign air:
"Espresso, cappuchino or latte?"

But Temple Bar is like a Wild West Show,
all tits 'n' bums, the crowds have briefly trapped
the Rector's son in some Dantean scene...

Inside, he reads the one he thinks they'll know:
the drunkenness of things seems more than apt,
the more-than-plate-glass window in between.

Amber's Epiphany

Was it Christmas Eve you came,
"the worst time of the year"
and nobody speaking of snow?
We were all on our best behaviour,
trying to live up to your name,
Amber —between 'stop' and 'go'.

But O the icing on the cake:
when you removed your shoulder wrap
and bright tattoos shone all around,
shepherds and wise men, nudged awake,
drew nigh to view that starry map;
the cat knelt on the ground.

Give & Take

for Eoin

What would I give
to hold you again
in the crook of my left arm
and have you hold on for dear life
to the lobe of my left ear?

What would you take
to hold me again
in the crook of your left arm
and have me hold on for dear life
to the lobe of your left....
No, I mean the right....
the one that is not pierced!

A Measured Response

for Eoin

I want to give you, son, a sense
of how it was pre-metrication:
£-s-d, pounds, shillings and pence;
florins, farthings and huge half-crowns;
a thruppenny bit (now that was money!);
a pint of milk, four quarts a gallon;
two ounces, please, of dolly mixtures;
there's eight stones in a hundredweight;
two thousand, two hundred and forty pounds
in a ton; one thousand, seven hundred and sixty
yards to the mile—squared's how many acres?
No matter. Now you appreciate
why I've got your shirt in my clinch,
ranting about "one bloody inch!"

Centesimal

Or 100 words for 'Poetry Ireland Review 100'

All the way from Buckingham
The centenarian's kissogram.

Minus forty in the shade
When Fahrenheit meets Centigrade.

No entomologist would cede
The bold claim of the centipede.

Not an inch! is certainly neater
Than *not 2.5 centimetre!*

No need to go all Mensa-mental
To guess how many pounds in a cental.

How long did Colorado wait
Before it became The Centennial State?

Leafing through the inventory
Of the *Sale of the Century.*

The money came, the money went;
Don't give a *dam*, don't care a cent.

One hundred ways to count your loss,
Centurion at the foot of The Cross.

Proverbs for the Computer Age

An Apple a day keeps the hacker away

Baud news travels fast

Better to light one Intel than to cursor the darkness

When the mat's away the mouse will play

Necessity is the motherboard of invention

Every blog has its day

Fight virus with virus

All that twitters is not scrolled

Let sleeping laptops lie

Beware of geeks bearing gifs

The Scientific Question

for Dietz

Adolf Ferdinand Reinhold,
inventor of the thermos flask,
explains to God the virtues of
his silvered, glass-walled vacuum:
"The boiling oil of Hell below
(from which Yourself preserve me!)
my flask will keep it hot till Kingdom come;
ice-water from sweet Heaven above
(so cool on Dives' burning tongue)
my flask will keep it cold eternally".
Before the great *Te Deum* is sung
the Devil interrupts to ask:
"My dear Professor, hot *and* cold?—
how on earth does it know?"

The Principle of Narcissus

After the first, fierce glance,
the kiss-kiss mouth, half-smile half-frown,
comes the slowly dawning fact:
that he can see his self reversed
from left to right and vice versa
but not (apparently) upside down
is less a matter of symmetry
(two each of arm, of leg, of eye ...)
and more his way of entering
his image in the earthbound act
of one-two-three-and- dance;
until he takes the vaulter's spring,
the leap of faith, the mad head ov-
er heels in love.

On the Determination of the Golden Ratio ϕ by a Series of Theatrical Approximations

for The Golden Gang

The Golden What? [ϕ= ∞] *Nonsense!*

Stairs, calipers, geometry & tea [ϕ= 1.000] *Wrong!*

Pyramids, flagellation of Christ,
Yeats, Blu-Tack, a plan, a list [ϕ= 2.000] *Poor!*

Barabbalab, Bridge, Spike,
red nose sphere, some tyke
whips the director's bike [ϕ= 1.500] *Average!*

The set of all possible sets;
stage lights, strings and frets;
the Eye of God
getting the nod;
a touch of your Swami Beck-etts [ϕ= 1.666] *Improving!*

This vanishing trope
of Indian rope,
a luminous spiral,
right-handed chiral
held with the aid
of stiff metal braid:
O make it your stop,
the local Pound Shop [ϕ= 1.600] *Better!*

Dazzling bright
Vitruvian kit
of LED lights;

poet's keep-fit
barefoot in park;
camera-shy
need not apply;
leap in the dark,
finding his mark;
—Wheel, Cather*ine!*
—Sire, depend on it;
just the one line
short of a sonnet [ϕ= 1.625] *Close!*

'Pythagoras planned it,' as the poet said.
'Ulster says Noh'—the masked sage.
Simon & Garf: 'Is the theatre really dead?'
      Cube: love's dearth.
      Colour it blue.
      Melancholic—Earth.
            Icosohedron: splutter.
            Colour it green.
            Phlegmatic—Water.
                  Octahedron: wondrous fair.
                  Colour it yellow.
                  Sanguine—Air.
                        Tetrahedron: desire.
                        Colour it red.
                        Choleric—Fire.
                              Dodecahedron: either/either.
                              Colour it black or white,
                              to be determined—Aether.
While I stand here like some 'apprentice mage',
upon my soul, you'll see a Golden Dawn
before I take this 'free play' off the stage [ϕ= 1.615] *Done?*

The Longest Day

Began with a good night's sleep,
sweet-dreaming order from chaos:
"O the first three minutes!"
Then, over coffee and croissants,
what I shall call 'life' appears,
a slow pot distillation
that lasts until well after dinner,
all limpid, landless, still.
Now, curled up by the fire
with a book from the library,
my goodness, just look at the time!
At twenty-three fifty-eight-and-a-half,
something comes crawling out of the woodwork,
and a mere two seconds to midnight,
in my own image & likeness,
the nightmare begins.

Weather Eye

One year into the latest ceasefire
it dawns on us: this could overtake
the weather as the one safe topic.
When fifty-one per cent (a clear
majority of those surveyed)
say "it'll not last", of course they mean
this long hot summer, dry-as-a-bone
gardens and who's got the energy
to coax kids from T-shirt 'n' sandals
back into school uniforms?
We rub our relics, hug our charms,
resume our raindance rituals,
aware that equally it must
fall on the evil and the just.

The Last Security Man in Ulster

He was funny, at first—boarding a bus
to march, arms swinging, down the aisle,
checking the luggage rack, under the seats,
getting off at the very next stop.
O harmless enough, if a bit irritating,
the way he'd hang around the porch
wanting to see inside the shopping,
giving the kids' schoolbags the wipe
with an army-issue metal detector.
(They'd never bothered to ask for it back.)
But when he frisked the new home-help
and pitched the alarm-clock through the window
we served him with a watchamacallit—
that's it, an exclusion order.

Ode to the Hills Hoist

for Susannah & Craig

Not every man returns from war
with a head full of laundry: an echo, perhaps,
of his predecessors who hung out, sang out,
more than just their ragged washing
on the rusty Siegfried Line.
A backyard Sydney Harbour Bridge
of swords not beaten into ploughshares
but into a V-for-Victory sign,
complete with rack and pinion drive
to cause the whitened sheets to flap
as high as a flag on top of a ridge—
for all the world like a radar dish
trying to locate those who'd not
made it back alive.

Outback Haiku

More than it can bear
is its mislabelling as
the koala *bear.*

Lie on for a while
with no alarm clock swallowed—
the old crocodile.

Unseats this rider
dashing off a stirrup-cup—
the huntsman spider.

Is the flat earth theorem
the biggest breakthrough of the
giant flat earthworm?

"Bush tucker's awesome!"
issues from my wheelie bin—
the brushtail possum.

Just the wrong lingo
for chatting up city dogs—
the lonesome dingo.

No unarmed combat
is lightly engaged in by
the common wombat.

Diary most droll:
aged thirteen and three-quarters,
marsupial mole.

A search of the boot
for long-nosed pliers yields the
long-nosed bandicoot.

With its punk hairdo,
could be Nancy, could be Sid,
the white cockatoo.

"Tsk, tsk, tsk, poor you!"
the most sincere regrets of
the bush kangaroo.

Wellington Bob

What passable cup drove you to enter
my City Gallery poetry reading?
You were quiet until it was 'question time'
then ranted about 'The One', inviting
the audience to, as it were, go forth
and multiply—which I so richly
deserved for my lame joke that the rhyme
for 'death' in Yeats' epitaph
was not really 'breath' but 'meth'.
In brewery tones you confide in me
that you can hear police bullhorns:
they cry out "Bob, Bob, heal thyself,
come down from the cross of the Majestic Centre!"
The one with the post-post-modern crown of thorns.

South Island

for Peter Kuch

Contrast "one country, two islands!"
with my "one island, two countries?"
When, in the murdering seventies
I finally put up my hands
(having lived it, in Mahon's gloss,
bomb by bomb) and went south,
I was homesick, twisting my mouth
to chew on their soft vowel *blas.*

The sign at a Christchurch store—
Just in, Midget Gems!— greets
me kindly, calling me forth
to a home-coming, glen to shore
and the hamely tongue's wee sweets:
South Island, peaceable North.